The bond between parent and son
is a special one.
It remains unchanged by time or distance.
It is the purest love —
unconditional and true...
It is a gift held in the heart and in the soul.

~ Stephanie Douglass

A Son

Is Life's Greatest Gift

Words of Love and Advice for a Son Any Parent Would Be Proud Of

A Blue Mountain Arts® Collection

Edited by Patricia Wayant

Blue Mountain Press™

Boulder, Colorado

We wish to thank Susan Polis Schutz for permission to reprint the following poems that appear in this publication: "Son, You Continue to Amaze Me," "I Hope Your Dreams Become a Reality," and "I hope that you always keep your wonderful attitude...." Copyright © 1985, 1988, 1992 by Stephen Schutz and Susan Polis Schutz. And for "Whether You Are Near or Far, Son...." Copyright © 1980 by Continental Publications. All rights reserved.

Library of Congress Control Number: 2015909988
ISBN: 978-1-59842-908-4

Acknowledgments appear on page 92.

M and Blue Mountain Press are registered in U.S. Patent and Trademark Office. Certain trademarks are used under license.

Printed in China.
First Printing: 2015

✪ This book is printed on recycled paper.

This book is printed on paper that has been specially produced to be acid free (neutral pH) and contains no groundwood or unbleached pulp. It conforms with all the requirements of the American National Standards Institute, Inc., so as to ensure that this book will last and be enjoyed by future generations.

Blue Mountain Arts, Inc.

P.O. Box 4549, Boulder, Colorado 80306

Contents

(Authors listed in order of first appearance)

My Son

You didn't grow up all at once,
although sometimes it seems
it was only yesterday that
I cradled you
in my arms as you slept.
Now that you're taller than I am
and your own arms can lift
the heaviest weight with ease,
I just want you to know
how much pride it has brought me
to watch you grow
stronger each year.
I'm even prouder
you've developed other kinds
of strength, such as honesty
    and responsibility.

I'm proud of your intelligence
and the thoughtful way you make decisions.
I'm proud of your determination,
your character, and the way you persevere.
I'm proud of the kindness
and respect you show to others
and of their admiration for you in return.
And although I'll always love you
no matter what,
what really makes me beam
is the realization that you've grown
into the amazing young man
I dreamed you'd become all those years ago,
when I cradled you in my arms as you slept.

~ *Jody Arlene*

I Truly Cherish
Our Relationship

When I first held you,
you didn't need to do anything
to make me love you;
you were the most precious thing
I'd ever seen.
As the years went by...
you grew into the precious little boy
who could melt my heart
with just a smile,
and the bond between us grew.
It seemed the more love I gave,
the more God replenished it,
and as the years went by,
I found a thousand reasons
to love you even more.

Now... I look at the strong,
amazing man you've become —
and it fills me with so much joy.
I hope you know how much
I appreciate you
and cherish the beautiful
relationship we share.

∼ Jason Blume

You Mean So Much to Me

Sometimes I can hardly believe
that the man I see
    when I look at you
used to be my little boy.
Where did the time go?
How did the moments turn into years
that disappeared behind us
at such great speed?
I am in awe at the changes that
have taken place in you,
and sometimes it saddens me
because that part of my life is over.
Yet I also feel the happiness and pride
in having a son who is all grown up,
and nothing can dull or dampen
the wonderful memories I have
of you as my little boy.
Even the rough times, the trying times,
and the overwhelming times
have sweetened through the years.
Memories of you still bring
laughter and delight,
a warmness of heart,
and tears to my eyes.

The pride I have in you
and the love I feel for you
have continued to grow, much like you have.
You are even more precious to me now
than you were before.
If you could look inside my heart
and see the love there,
if you could feel its strength and depth,
then you would know that you
have fulfilled my life in ways
no other person ever could.

~ Barbara Cage

There was a time
when I could hold you close,
give you a hug of reassurance,
guide you through life's storms,
and keep you safe and sheltered.
Now... you make those big decisions.
You alone decide which path to take,
what choice to make, how things will go.
But I want you to know that even though
I can't always calm your fears,
hold you in a safe embrace,
or give your life direction...
I am still here with open arms.
I will always have
a special hug for you
and all the time in the world to listen.

~ Barbara J. Hall

We Are Family

A family is... the sweetest feelings ~ The
warmest hugs ~ Trust and togetherness ~
Unconditional love ~ The stories of our
lives written on the same page ~ The
nicest memories anyone has ever made ~
Treasured photos ~ Thankful tears ~ Hearts
overflowing with all the years ~ Being there
for one another ~ Supporting and caring ~
Understanding ~ Helping ~ Sharing ~
Walking life's path together, and making the
journey more beautiful because...

We are a family...
and a family
is love.
~ Marin McKay

The Bond Between Parent and Son Lasts a Lifetime

The bond between parent and son
    is a special one.
It remains unchanged by time or distance.
It is the purest love —
    unconditional and true.
It is understanding of any situation
and forgiving of any mistake.
It creates a support that is constant
while everything else changes.
It is a friendship based on mutual
    love, respect,
and a genuine liking of each other
    as a person.
It is knowing that no matter where
    you go or who you are,
there is someone who truly loves you
and is always there to support and
    console you.
When a situation seems impossible,
you make it through together
by holding on to each other.

The bond between parent and son
is strong enough to withstand harsh words
    and hurt feelings,
for it is smart enough to always
see the love beyond the words.
It is brave enough to always speak the truth,
even when lies would be easier.
It is always there — anytime, anywhere —
whenever it is needed.
It is a gift held in the heart and in the soul,
and it cannot be taken away
or exchanged for another.
To possess this love is a treasure
that makes life more valuable.

~ Stephanie Douglass

Son, You Continue to Amaze Me

To see you happy —
laughing and joking
smiling and content
striving toward goals of your own
accomplishing what you set out to do
having fun
capable of loving and being loved
is what I always wished for you

Today I thought about your
    handsome face
and felt your excitement for life
and your genuine happiness
and I, as your parent
    burst with pride
as I realized that my dreams
    for you have come true
What an extraordinary person
    you have become
and as you continue to grow
please remember always
how very much
I love you
                    ~ Susan Polis Schutz

What Is a Son?

A son is a warm spot in your heart and a smile on your lips.

In the beginning he is charmingly innocent, putting his complete trust in you.

He comes to you for a hand to hold and for the security only your arms can provide.

He shares his tales of adventure and knows how proud you are of his discoveries and accomplishments.

All his problems can be solved by a hug and a kiss from you, and the bond you share is so strong it is almost tangible.

Time passes, and your innocent little boy starts to test his limits. He lets go of your hand to race into the midst of life without thinking ahead or looking both ways.

His problems have grown along with him, and he has learned that you can't always make his life better or kiss his troubles away.

He spends much of his time away from you, and though you long for the closeness you once shared, he chooses independence and privacy.

Discoveries and accomplishments aren't as easy
to come by now, and sometimes he wonders
about his worth.

But you know the worth of that young man. He
is your past and your future. He is hopes and
dreams that have made it through each and
every disappointment and failure.

In your heart, your son is precious and treasured.
Together, you struggled through the years trying
to find the right amount of independence for each
new stage of his life, until finally, you had to
learn to let him go.

Now you put your trust in him, leaving that son,
whom you hold so dear, totally in his own care.
You hope he always remembers that you have
a hand for him to hold and arms to provide
comfort or support.

Most of all, you hope that he believes in himself
as much as you believe in him and that he
knows how much you love him.

~ Barbara Cage

I Hope Your Dreams
Become a Reality

Dreams can come true if you take the time to
think about what you want in life...
Get to know yourself
Find out who you are
Choose your goals carefully
Be honest with yourself
Find many interests and pursue them
Find out what is important to you
Find out what you are good at
Don't be afraid to make mistakes
Work hard to achieve successes
When things are not going right
don't give up — just try harder
Find courage inside of you to remain strong
Give yourself freedom to try out new things
Don't be so set in your ways that you can't grow
Always act in an ethical way
Laugh and have a good time
Form relationships with people you respect
Treat others as you want them to treat you

Be honest with people
Accept the truth
Speak the truth
Open yourself up to love
Don't be afraid to love
Remain close to your family
Take part in the beauty of nature
Be appreciative of all that you have
Help those less fortunate than you
Try to make other lives happy
Work toward peace in the world
Live life to the fullest

~ Susan Polis Schutz

Remember that a wish
can take you anywhere —
and half the fun is reaching for a star.
Your dreams were made to soar;
let your spirit dance
in every waking moment.
Every day comes bearing gifts;
hold each promise in your hands.
Within you is your very own universe.
A bit of stardust is blowing your way —
a bit of light and a bit of wonder.
Follow your leanings;
listen to the whispers of your soul.

~ Linda E. Knight

Believe

Believe in everything
you set out to do.
Believe in yourself
right down to your shoes.

Believe in wishes made
on falling stars
and whispered into fountains.

Fall in love with a dream.
Keep it with you every day.
Let it grow to be
bigger than the sun.

You have magic inside you —
imagination, heart, and soul.
Believe in yourself,
believe in your dream,
and you can go anywhere
and you can do anything.

~ Charley Knox

The road to greatness starts within you.
Count your blessings,
cherish your potential,
and appreciate the full beauty
of every day.
Tomorrow is yours to create.
There's so much potential inside you...
in every dream you hold close
and in each hope that is important to you.
Dance your way to the stars,
dream tomorrow into being,
and celebrate each step along the way.
Expect great things,
and they will be yours someday.

~ Linda E. Knight

The measure of a man is not found in
the things he owns
or what he's saved for retirement
or even his accomplishments.

The true measure of a man is found in
    his faith and his heart.
It's found in the friends who stand by him,
the strength he displays under pressure,
the sensitivity he unashamedly expresses,
and his willingness to reveal vulnerability,
    even at the risk of being hurt.

And it's found in the truth of his words,
    the genuineness of his life,
    his unselfish actions,
    and the values he lives by.

                              ～ Craig Brannon

Eleven Lessons for My Son

These are lessons that I have both learned and am still learning... And as you discover new truths, please be sure to share them with me, as my fervent hope has always been that the student surpasses the teacher.

I. *The definition of money.* You are gaining perspective on what is needed financially in this world. I implore you to remember that money isn't what you think it is. Contrary to popular belief, money isn't the answer to all your problems; things purchased with money don't matter in the long-term, because they can be lost, stolen, broken, or taken away. What money enables is freedom and flexibility, both for you and for those around you.

2. *Fear and failure.* Don't be afraid of failure. Fear will paralyze and control you. Those who are afraid to fail are also afraid to succeed. To accomplish anything, you must risk losing in order to capture what you want. It is our struggles that not only define us, but also cause our growth. Remember: you will win some, and you will lose some, but either way you are loved for just being you.

3. *Want and need.* Sure, you're going to need a job and a paycheck. But don't lose sight of what you truly *want* from life, trading your wants for what you *need*. As you get older, you will regret so few decisions that you made, and instead will experience profound remorse about the decisions that you *didn't* make and the opportunities you *didn't* pursue. Don't live a life of "What If"; instead, take chances.

4. *Love hard.* You can't control what another person does or says — you can only control you. If you love someone, love them completely. Don't hold back out of fear. If you do, you will never know what might have happened. Sure, it might not work out, but don't let that be because you were ruled by fear...

5. *Be kind.* **You will never know what another person's experience has been. As such, please remember to be empathetic and compassionate.**

6. *Do much.* **Learn, grow, experience, change, shift, adjust — and then change again. Do as much as you can and experience all you are able. Life is not measured by how fast you arrive at the end, because none of us are going to make it out of this alive. Life is about the accumulation of what you know, what you did, what you learned, and what you thought about through it all.**

7. *Give.* **Be giving with your time, your knowledge, your money, your effort, your love, and yourself. You are a gift to the world and you should share.**

8. *Always dream.* **There are times to be a realist, but not at the expense of passion. Dream big and chase what you want. Don't allow anyone to tell you that your dreams are too big.**

9. Don't grow up. At various points in your life, you will need to be an adult and make hard decisions. However, being an adult doesn't mean that you are forced to grow up. Make sure you still act like a kid whenever possible; life is immensely more fun that way.

10. Be brave. As a man, you will face challenging times; it happens to all of us. What defines you is how you respond to that adversity. It's normal to be scared — just don't stop moving forward.

11. Be you. Don't allow anyone to define who you are. You are an incredible, vibrant, resourceful, amazing, talented, tenacious, outstanding, and courageous young man. As you get exposed to new things and lessons, your perspective will shift, but you do the shifting. Don't hand over the definition of who you are to anyone else. You choose who you are, what you stand for, and what you believe in.

~ *Charles J. Orlando*

Remember What Is Most Important...

It's not having everything go right;
it's facing whatever goes wrong.
It's not being without fear;
it's having the determination
   to go on in spite of it.
It's not where you stand,
but the direction you're going in.
It's more than never having bad moments;
it's knowing you are always
   bigger than the moment.
It's believing you have already
   been given everything
you need to handle life.
It's not being able to rid
   the world of all its injustices;
it's being able to rise above them.
It's the belief in your heart
   that there will always be
more good than bad in the world.

Remember to live just this one day
and not add tomorrow's troubles
    to today's load.
Remember that every day ends
and brings a new tomorrow
full of exciting new things.
Love what you do,
    do the best you can,
and always remember
    how much you are loved.

~ Vickie M. Worsham

In life, there will be times when you're going to need so much courage. There will be times... when you'll feel like crying yourself to sleep. When your confidence is shaken. When you're scared, angry, and confused. When you can't believe this is happening to you.

But for every one of those situations, there will also be times when you look deep inside and realize... you're going to be okay.

There will be times when you find out that you're such a fighter. When you discover how strong you really can be and that you're truly a survivor.

The people with the biggest hearts are the ones who can be most vulnerable sometimes. But they're also the ones who have the capacity to hold on tight and find a way through.

You're one of those people.

~ *Terry Bairnson*

When You're Thankful
for Your Troubles,
They Can Become Blessings

Be thankful that you don't already have
everything you desire.
If you did, what would there be to look forward to?
Be thankful when you don't know something,
for it gives you the opportunity to learn.
Be thankful for the difficult times.
During those times, you grow.
Be thankful for your limitations,
because they give you opportunities for improvement.

Be thankful for each new challenge,
because it will build your strength and character.
Be thankful for your mistakes.
They will teach you valuable lessons.
Be thankful when you're tired and weary,
because it means you've made an effort.
It's easy to be thankful for the good things.
A life of rich fulfillment comes to those who
    are also thankful for the setbacks.
Gratitude can turn a negative into a positive.
Find a way to be thankful for your troubles,
and they can become your blessings.

~ *Author Unknown*

A Positive Attitude Shapes Your World

The way you think shapes your world.
A positive attitude can open
the door to limitless possibilities.
When you give yourself
the freedom to dream and imagine,
your world expands.
The impossible becomes possible.
So breathe in peace and hope,
and give your dreams a chance.
Remember, transformation
is not only possible,
it happens every day;
think of butterflies, seeds,
and springtime.

*Our world is full of new beginnings.
It is larger than any of us can comprehend.
Take heart, believe in big skies
and wide-open spaces,
and hold on to the promise
of mysteries and magic.
There is space for your dreams to grow.
The future may astonish you.*

~ Rebecca Brown

The Answers You Seek
Are Inside of You

Inside of you lie all the answers.
Any worries and confusion you harbor
    as you walk through your life each day
don't have to weigh you down
    and close you off from the true you...
because all the answers lie
    within your soul.

Listen to your heart.
Hear your spirit as it guides you
to the next positive step toward
    your freedom.
Hear your mind's voice leading you
    in the right direction.
You will never lead yourself wrong.

You've got to believe in yourself,
in your strength,
and in your ability to navigate life's paths.
Don't doubt yourself for a moment.
Move forward with surety and grace
and never look back.

The vision for your life is yours.
Reach for it...
grasp it...
and it will be yours.

~ Paula Michele Adams

What It Means to Be a Man

A man is someone who realizes
　　that strength of character
is more important than being tough.

He can be tender and kind,
　　and he doesn't misuse his authority.
He is generous and enjoys
　　giving as well as receiving.
He is understanding;
　　he tries to see both sides
　　　　of a situation.

He is responsible;
  he knows what needs to be done,
    and he does it.
He is trustworthy;
  his word is his honor.
He loves humor and looks
  at the bright side of things.
He takes time to think before he reacts.
He loves life, nature, discovery,
  excitement, and so much more.
He is a little boy sometimes,
  living in an adult body
and enjoying the best of both worlds.

                              ~ *Barbara Cage*

Sometimes a Son

Sometimes a son
will surprise you   come to sit
on the side of your bed
where you lie with a broken leg
everyone else seems to have forgotten
He will balance three pieces
of grape smeared toast
on a too small plate   drink orange juice
from your best crystal   You don't mind
this particular morning   the first sun
flashing off the leaves outside your window
He will tell you his funniest stories
fragments of toast   crumbling
onto the sheets   You will not brush them away
Your son will tell you these things
you've heard before
They will seem new now   as beside you he
shakes your whole bed with his laughter

~ Janice Townley Moore

*S*on, my favorite memories all have reflections of you in them. And I know how it feels to love someone with all my heart... because that's how I love you.

There are probably far too many things in my life that I take for granted. But you will never, ever be one of them. I *know* how blessed I am to have you here, and I can't help thinking of what utter and absolute joy I would have missed... if I hadn't had the gift... of you in my life.

~ Douglas Pagels

I'm So Proud of You!

I remember watching you
take your first unsteady steps,
your legs wobbly and unsure.
I wanted to catch you,
protect you, and keep you safe,
but soon your steps became steadier,
and you ran farther and farther from me.
I loved watching you grow
more independent and mature,
even as you became
more separate and individual.

Now I watch you take
your first steps into the world.
A more vast and rich tapestry awaits you
than the carpet of our family room
and the tiles of our kitchen floor.
Though I still want
to pull you to me to keep you safe,
I want you to know I am so proud
of the tremendous person
you have become.
You have my love,
my pride, and my respect.
As I watch you venture out into
this new, exciting stage of life,
I know your steps
will become sure-footed,
and soon you will be
running once more toward
the infinite possibilities
you can dream for yourself.

~ Jessica Dainty Johns

I Love You Exactly
as You Are

One day you will want to know
that someone in this world
thinks the sun rises when you smile
and that nothing is as amazing as
    your laugh.
If ever you feel the burden of
    guilt or failure and believe
        that no one
could love you just the way you are,
just know that I do.
Every second you are with me
is a gift no one could ever
put a price on.
You are the reason why
my life is so wonderful.

           ~ Renate M. Braddy

I hope that you always keep
your wonderful attitude
that whatever happens
in your life
happens for the best
I hope that you are always
truly happy and thankful
for whatever you have
and that you never care
about what you do not have
You are a very rare person
and I am so proud
to have you as my son
You cannot imagine
how happy you make me
I do not have to worry
about you at all
You are everything
a parent could wish for
I love you very much

$\sim$ Susan Polis Schutz

What Being Your Parent Means to Me

Being your parent means that I have had the opportunity to experience loving someone more than I love myself. I have learned what it's like to experience joy and pain through someone else's life.

Being your parent hasn't always been easy, and I'm sure I've said and done things that have hurt or confused you. But no one has ever made me as satisfied as you do just by being happy. No one has made me as proud as you do just by living up to your responsibilities.

No one's smile has ever warmed my heart like yours does; no one's laughter fills my heart with delight as quickly as yours can. No one's hugs feel as sweet, and no one's dreams mean as much to me as yours do.

No other memories of bad times have miraculously turned into important lessons or humorous stories; the good times have become precious treasures to relive again and again.

You are a part of me, and no matter what happened in the past or what the future holds, you are someone I will always accept, forgive, appreciate, adore, and love unconditionally.

Being your parent means that I've been given one of life's greatest gifts: you.

~ Barbara Cage

Always Be True to Yourself

There is no one in the past, present, or future who will ever offer the world what you do. No one will think, act, or smile exactly like you. No one will be able to come up with your unique points of view.

Don't hold back who you really are. When you are true to yourself, you glow. When you are passionate about your dreams, you shine. When you live fully, people are drawn to you. And then you can't help but make friends with good people: the ones who love you for just being you.

~ April Aragam

You are not your car. You are not your job. You are not your bank account. These things are useful, and they help you to make your way through the world, but they do not define you.

You are not your problems. You are not your failures. You are not your disappointments. These things challenge you and can ultimately help you to grow, but they do not have to limit you.

You are the child who danced in the sunshine, the young person who dreamed of changing the world. You are the admirer of all the beauty around you, a spirit who cannot be tied down. You are the best that you can imagine, a bundle of possibilities yearning to be fulfilled.

The shallow, superficial things will define or limit you only to the extent that you let them. Pay attention to them, but don't give your life to them. You are so much more.

~ *Ralph S. Marston, Jr.*

Be Someone
Others Look Up To

Be someone others admire
for the life that you lead and
the kindness that is such a
sweet and natural part of you...

for the way you treat other people...

for how easily a smile finds its way
to your face...

for the work that you do and the
places your journeys take you...

*for your dedication to all the right
things and your devotion to
your family...*

*for how completely you care and
how willingly you are always there
for the people who need you...*

*for being the light that you are...
in the lives of others.*
$\sim$ *L. N. Mallory*

Let Your Passion Guide You

You will not find happiness by living someone else's dream. Put aside what others think you "should" do, and allow your passion, enthusiasm, and exuberance to be your guide. Identify those interests that stimulate you, challenge you, excite you, and fulfill you. Explore how you might translate your passions into attainable goals.

What do you love to do? How would you spend your time if money were no object?

The more you are emotionally connected to your pursuit, the more willing you will be to continue on your path — even through the inevitable challenges. Choose goals that emanate from your heart and make you excited.

~ Jason Blume

Remember...
It's not how much you accomplish in life
that really counts,
but how much you give to others.
It's not how high you build your dreams
that makes a difference,
but how high your faith can climb.
It's not how many goals you reach,
but how many lives you touch.
It's not who you know that matters,
but who you are inside.

Live each day to its fullest potential,
and you can make a difference
    in the world.
                    ~ Rebecca Barlow Jordan

Winners Take Chances

Like everyone else, winners fear failing,
but they refuse to let fear control them.
Winners don't give up.
When life gets rough, they hang in
until the going gets better.
Winners are flexible.
They realize there is more than one way
and are willing to try others.
Winners know they are not perfect.
They respect their weaknesses
while making the most of their strengths.
Winners fall, but they don't stay down.
They stubbornly refuse to let a fall
        keep them from climbing.

Winners don't blame
fate for their failures
or luck for their successes.
Winners accept responsibility
for their lives.
Winners are positive thinkers
who see good in all things.
From the ordinary, they make
the extraordinary.
Winners believe in the path they
have chosen
even when it's hard,
even when others can't see
where they are going.
Winners are patient.
They know a goal is only as worthy
as the effort that's required
to achieve it.

~ Nancye Sims

What It Really Means to Be a Success

You are a success... if you are true to yourself; if you are welcoming to people of all varieties; and if you showcase the strength of every member of your team.

You are a success... if you can lead in a crisis and keep hearts serene; if you can smile at your critics and carry on peacefully; if you can take a tumble and stand up smiling gracefully; if you can weigh the pros and cons of every decision.

If you live your values, act responsibly, and give back to your community; if you try to strengthen your family ties, keep alive precious traditions, and record your family history for future generations... you are a success.

You are a success... if you always remember where you came from and help the people who are still climbing the ladder to a better life; if you are generous in your praise, fair in your criticism, and moderate in the amount of advice you give.

If you realize that you still have a lot to learn and miles to go before you find the answers you seek; if you are ready to do everything it takes to live your life to the fullest... then whatever path you take, you will find success.

~ Jacqueline Schiff

The Secret to a Happy Life

There are three distinct periods
in everyone's life:
the past, the present, and the future.
The secret to a happy life
is to remember the best moments
of the past, for they are your treasures;
to live in the present moment
and make each one truly memorable;
and to not be concerned
about the future,
for no one can know for certain
what it will bring.

Right now is for making sound choices,
for mingling with those who give you joy,
and for doing what brings you satisfaction.
Right now is a collection of moments
that will never happen again.

Live one day at a time
and live it brilliantly,
for the things you do today
become treasures to store
in your trove...
and the future will arrive tomorrow
anyway.

~ Perri Elizabeth Hogan

Life isn't about keeping score. It's not about how many people call you, and it's not about who you've dated, are dating, or haven't dated at all.

It isn't about who you've kissed, what sport you play, or which guy or girl likes you. It's not about your shoes or your hair or the color of your skin or where you live or go to school. In fact, it's not about grades, money, clothes, or colleges that accept you or not.

Life isn't about if you have lots of friends or if you are alone, and it's not about how accepted or not accepted you are. Life just isn't about that.

But life is about who you love and who you hurt. It's about how you feel about yourself. It's about trust, happiness, and compassion. It's about sticking up for your friends and replacing inner hate with love.

Life is about avoiding jealousy, overcoming ignorance, and building confidence. It's about what you say and what you mean. It's about seeing people for who they are and not what they have.

Most of all, life is about choosing to use your life to touch someone else's in a way that could never have been achieved otherwise. These choices are what life's about.

~ *Adam Fendelman*

These Are Things
I Want You
to Remember

Each of us is unique and talented in our own
way. When the skies are dark and hope seems far
away, I want you to remember there's something
good awaiting you just around the corner...
if only you keep going. Learn to love yourself
unconditionally and to be patient and kind.

There will be times in your life when the path
ahead is unclear. I want you to remember that
no matter which road you choose, there will be
wonderful adventures to have and new friends
to meet, so allow yourself to grow and let new
experiences enrich your life. Don't think you must
know all the answers right now. Let life take you
to unknown territory. Feel free to explore.

I want you to remember that it's okay to make mistakes, even big ones. From each failing we grow stronger. Don't let others' ideas of perfection bring you down. Take the time to learn about yourself and what you really like. Make your life count.

There will be people who doubt your potential and ability, but let there be a safe place inside you that no one can touch. I want you to always remember how spectacular you are, just by being you.

~ Genevieve Leslie

What You Need to Know About Love

The world is full of love; there is no end to it. And if you have it in your life, you'll find yourself capable of achieving great things.

Remember there are many different kinds of love; don't neglect any of them, for each will add something different and unique to your days. Open yourself to every experience, and don't be afraid to reveal your feelings. If it's in your nature to be a romantic, allow yourself to fully and freely express it; you may discover talents and gifts within you that you never could have found in any other way.

Don't ever let the actions of other people lead you to shut off your own emotions or hesitate to put your faith in love. Give your relationships the very best that's in you — remembering as you do that all the love you give away just increases your own capacity for receiving even more in return someday.

Always look at the world with loving eyes, and you'll find love reflected back to you from every corner of your days. Your heart can be a catalyst for changing the world as long as you treat everyone you meet in kind and loving ways.

Remember it is your destiny to be a strong, loving, happy man — and you will be, if you always walk the path of life with an open and trusting heart and give yourself to love.

~ Avery Jakobs

Love is something eternal — the aspect may change, but not the essence. There is the same difference in a person before and after he is in love as there is in an unlighted lamp and one that is burning. The lamp was there and it was a good lamp, but now it is shedding light, too, and that is its real function.

~ Vincent van Gogh

Love is the miracle that can take two lives and mold them into one, take two souls and bind them for life, take two hearts and fill them with enough passion and tenderness to last a lifetime.

Love is a blessing that will lead you down life's most beautiful path.

~ *Michele Weber*

Whether You Are Near or Far, Son...
I Am Always Beside You

I will support you
in all that you
do
I will help you
in all that you
need
I will share with you
in all that you
experience
I will encourage you
in all that you
try
I will understand you
in all that is in your
heart
I will love you
in all that you
are

~ Susan Polis Schutz

You are the poem
I dreamed of writing,
the masterpiece
I longed to paint.
You are the shining star
I reached for in my
ever hopeful quest
for life fulfilled.
You are my child.
Now with all things
I am blessed.

~ Author Unknown

I Always Knew
I Couldn't Keep You
Small Forever

I took a lot of photographs
and wrote down all your "firsts,"
but there was no way to keep you
    small forever.
I have to admit that there are many days
when I miss that little boy.
Yet when I take a good look at the man
    you have become,
I see a strong, intelligent, wonderful
    human being,
and I am so proud.
You took to heart the things you learned
    when you were young,
and they have served you well.
Sharing and caring,
consideration and concern,
modesty and humility are all
    significant elements of who you are.

You speak your mind with respect for others.
You set great examples for people to follow.
You are reliable and trustworthy,
    which are such admirable traits.
Your life is full and rich and busy,
and I am so proud of all you have achieved.
I want you to remember that no matter
where you are or what you're doing,
I'm thinking of you with a heart full of love.
From the moment you were born
    and for the rest of our lives,
I feel so blessed to have you as my son.

~ Perri Elizabeth Hogan

In My Mind, You Will Always Be My Little Boy

I can't call you my little boy anymore, but you know you are, no matter your size or age. It doesn't matter how tall and strong and confident and brave you are. I see the man in you, but you are also my child, and nothing can ever change that. And if I glow whenever I say your name, it is because I love you beyond measure.

Son, you have taught me so many lessons, like that maturity isn't always related to age and that being a good listener can turn big problems into small ones. I look at you and smile at the memories, but I look forward to the future, bright with promise, because I know that whatever road you walk, a part of me walks beside you to keep you safe.

I know you are all grown up and very capable of standing on your own two feet to meet the day. You are the kind of man other men want to be... but to me you are still my little boy, always and forever.

~ *Lillie Franklin*

And So You Go

And so you go
out there, to life,
eager to leave the nest,
impatient to spread your wings.
In your face
there is such promise.
In your laugh, such nonchalance.
So much has changed,
yet there are moments —
    subliminal blips —
when I still see the toddler who,
    splayed in my lap or
        head snug against mine,
drank in one story after another,
whispered secrets in the dark,
spilled out kisses and laughs
    like a beneficent king.

There are moments
    when a pleased expression,
random outburst,
furrowed brow,
brings back a cherished glimpse
of that little boy lost.
In those moments,
it is hardest to say
farewell.
But I must,
and I can,
and I do —
then watch with pride and pain
through tears and years
of love.
And so you go.

~ Jayne Jaudon Ferrer

I Hope You'll Keep on Making Your Greatest Dreams Come True

You are bright, talented, and creative. You have a spirit of adventure and an intense desire to make the world better. You are sensitive to the needs of others and passionate about helping people. You are driven to reach dreams that will make your future so much brighter. You have an inner spark that kindles a light in everyone your life touches.

You are a precious gift to the present and the future, and you must never forget this. Keep on flying with your highest dreams, and believe they will carry you where you want to go. Say "yes" to challenges, and dare to make those big, bold dreams come true.

Tend the fires of your passions and use this energy to do good in life. Stand up for what is right. Protest the negative things in this world that damage the gifts of the heart. When you see a wrong, be strong in speaking out. Be committed in your friendships with those who need a friend the most. Be a volunteer and a positive leader.

Keep your good character, high ideals, and deepest passions alive and active. Fly on the wings of your talents and your mightiest dreams. Strive to change the world one day at a time. And as you fly, carry a picture of me smiling at you with my brightest love and my deepest pride.

~ *Jacqueline Schiff*

Never Forget
These Ten Things...

*Your happiness, health, and safety
mean everything to me.*

*No matter how old you get,
I will always think of you as my child
and love you as much as ever.*

*I enjoy being with you
and am very pleased at the person
you've turned out to be.*

*Your voice is one of my favorite sounds,
and your laughter always delights me.*

*You should always believe
that you are capable and worthy,
precious and unique —
and act accordingly.*

*You have touched my heart
and made me proud
more often than you could imagine.*

*Memories of you are very dear to me,
and sharing special times and traditions
makes them all the more enjoyable.*

*You bless my life in so many ways,
and I am thankful for the friendship
that we share.*

*There is nothing you could ever do
to lessen my love for you.*

*Being your parent has given me
happiness to the greatest degree
and warmth that fills my heart.
I am in awe that you came into my life
and made my dreams come true.*

~ Barbara Cage

I Would Do Anything for You

If I could bring you a world full of happiness,
I would. If I could take your sadness and pain
and feel them for you, I would. If I could give
you the strength to handle the problems that this
world may have for you, I'd do that too. There
is nothing that I wouldn't do for you to bring
laughter instead of tears into your life.

I can't give you happiness, but I can feel it with
you. I can't take away all your hurts in this
world, but I can share them with you. I can't
give you strength when you need it the most, but
I can try to be strong for you.

I can be there to tell you how much I love you. In times when you feel you need to reach out to someone, I can be there for you — not to change how you feel, but to go through it with you.

When you were little, I could hold you in my arms to comfort you, but you'll never be too grown up for me to put my arms around you. You are so very special to me, and the most precious gift I could have ever received was you on the day you were born.

~ Millie P. Lorenz

It's Been My Privilege to Witness You Grow Up

You are your own person, and I get to see what you choose to do with your time and talents. You may have started small and helpless in my arms, but now I know you are capable of so much. It has inspired me to watch you grow brilliantly into yourself. I have always had such high hopes for you, and you continue to exceed them with the incredible person you are.

When I look at you, I see years of memories and decades of potential. You have already changed my world in spectacular ways, and now I see you impact the rest of the world in wonderful ways as well. I am honored to be your parent.

But though I see the best parts of you, please know I never expect you to be perfect...
no one is. I am just so glad that you are perfectly you. I couldn't ask for more.

~ Amy L. Kuo

I Wish You
Life's Most Beautiful
Blessings...

I wish you a thankful heart, a resilient
and hopeful spirit, a tough resolve, and a
sensitivity to the needs of others.

I wish you confidence in yourself, self-respect,
imagination, and determination on the road
to success in achieving your goals.

May there be love in your life and a positive
attitude to guide you, along with wisdom,
awareness, and dreams to inspire you and
make you happy.

I wish you light when you're lost in the
darkness, clarity when you're confused, and
good common sense when you don't know
which way to go.

I wish you discipline and direction when you need to change something in your life and the good sense to deal with the things you can't change.

I wish you the faith of a little child although you're all grown up now.

I wish you sweet satisfaction in everything you do. May every kindness you've given to others be returned to you and fill you with happiness.

~ *Donna Fargo*

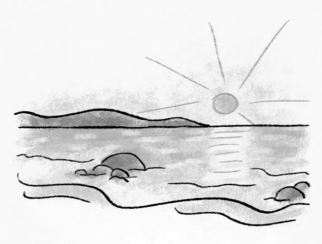

You Are Life's
Gift of Love to Me

You bring joy to my life and my heart.
You're such an amazing person
and a wonderful son.
You're the nicest gift
any parent could ever ask for.
All my prayers were answered
the day you were born.
I'm so thankful for every moment
and memory — even the tough ones.
You leave your own special "heartprint"
wherever you go.
You make a happy difference
in so many ways;
the universe is blessed to have you in it.
We've faced a few roadblocks now and then
and climbed our own share of mountains
a time or two.
Life hasn't always offered us an easy path,
but we didn't let that stop us;
we just went ahead and made our own way.

No one else has
your own brand of caring,
style of sharing,
and way of being
the wonderful son that you are.
No one else has a smile that can
light up a thousand tomorrows.
Your warmth can never be matched.
You truly are a gift of love to me.
I hope you will always
embrace the beauty of life,
hold your family close
and your dreams near,
and celebrate your blessings.
You make my world brighter
and my life sweeter.
Most of all, Son,
you make my heart smile.

~ Linda E. Knight

Everywhere You Journey in Life, Son, My Love Goes with You

Forever it will be with you: truly, joyfully, and more meant to be than words could ever say. You are the joy of my life, the source of my dearest memories, and the inspiration for my fondest wishes, and you are the sweetest present life could ever give to anyone.

I love you so much. I want you to remember that... every single day. And I want you to know that these are things I'll always hope and pray...

That the world will treat you fairly. That people will appreciate the one-in-a-million person you are. That you will be safe and smart and sure to make good choices on your journey through life. That a wealth of opportunities will come your way. That your blessings will be many, your troubles will be few, and that life will be very generous in giving you all the happiness and success you deserve.

You're not just a fantastic son. You're a tremendous, rare, and extraordinary person. All the different facets of your life — the ones you reveal to the rest of the world and the ones known only to those you're close to — are so impressive. And as people look even deeper, I know they can't help but see how wonderful you are inside.

I'll always love you, Son, with all my heart. And I couldn't be more proud of you... if I tried.

~ Douglas Pagels

ACKNOWLEDGMENTS

We gratefully acknowledge the permission granted by the following authors, publishers, and authors' representatives to reprint poems or excerpts from their publications.

Jason Blume for "I Truly Cherish Our Relationship" and "Let Your Passion Guide You." Copyright © 2013, 2014 by Jason Blume. All rights reserved.

Charles J. Orlando for "Eleven Lessons for My Son" from *Your Tango* (blog), June 14, 2014. Copyright © 2014 by Charles J. Orlando. All rights reserved.

Paula Michele Adams for "The Answers You Seek Are Inside of You." Copyright © 2015 by Paula Michele Adams. All rights reserved.

Finishing Line Press for "Sometimes a Son" from *Teaching the Robins* by Janice Townley Moore. Copyright © 2005 by Janice Townley Moore. All rights reserved.

April Aragam for "Always Be True to Yourself." Copyright © 2015 by April Aragam. All rights reserved.

The Daily Motivator, www.dailymotivator.com, for "You are not your car" from "You are more" by Ralph S. Marston, Jr. Copyright © 1999 by Ralph S. Marston, Jr. All rights reserved.

Jacqueline Schiff for "What It Really Means to Be a Success." Copyright © 2015 by Jacqueline Schiff. All rights reserved.

Perri Elizabeth Hogan for "The Secret to a Happy Life" and "I Always Knew I Couldn't Keep You Small Forever." Copyright © 2015 by Perri Elizabeth Hogan. All rights reserved.

Adam Fendelman, www.HollywoodChicago.com, for "Life isn't about keeping score" from "What Life Is All About." Copyright © 1996 by Adam Fendelman. All rights reserved. Reprinted by permission.

Genevieve Leslie for "These Are Things I Want You to Remember." Copyright © 2015 by Genevieve Leslie. All rights reserved.

Lillie Franklin for "In My Mind, You Will Always Be My Little Boy." Copyright © 2015 by Lillie Franklin. All rights reserved.

Jayne Jaudon Ferrer for "And So You Go" from *A Mother of Sons*. Copyright © 1996, 2004 by Jayne Jaudon Ferrer. All rights reserved.

PrimaDonna Entertainment Corp. for "I Wish You Life's Most Beautiful Blessings..." by Donna Fargo. Copyright © 2015 by PrimaDonna Entertainment Corp. All rights reserved.

A careful effort has been made to trace the ownership of selections used in this anthology in order to obtain permission to reprint copyrighted material and give proper credit to the copyright owners. If any error or omission has occurred, it is completely inadvertent, and we would like to make corrections in future editions provided that written notification is made to the publisher:

BLUE MOUNTAIN ARTS, INC., P.O. Box 4549, Boulder, Colorado 80306.